T0128918

# A Call to Love

## Nature's message for humanity to live with love

# A.C. TREMBLAY

**BALBOA**
PRESS

A DIVISION OF HAY HOUSE

Balboa Press books may be ordered through booksellers or by contacting:

Balboa Press
A Division of Hay House
1663 Liberty Drive
Bloomington, IN 47403
www.balboapress.com
1 (877) 407-4847

Because of the dynamic nature of the Internet, any web addresses or links contained in this book may have changed since publication and may no longer be valid. The views expressed in this work are solely those of the author and do not necessarily reflect the views of the publisher, and the publisher hereby disclaims any responsibility for them.

The author of this book does not dispense medical advice or prescribe the use of any technique as a form of treatment for physical, emotional, or medical problems without the advice of a physician, either directly or indirectly. The intent of the author is only to offer information of a general nature to help you in your quest for emotional and spiritual well-being. In the event you use any of the information in this book for yourself, which is your constitutional right, the author and the publisher assume no responsibility for your actions.

Any people depicted in stock imagery provided by Thinkstock are models, and such images are being used for illustrative purposes only. Certain stock imagery © Thinkstock.

Print information available on the last page.

ISBN: 978-1-5043-7806-2 (sc)
ISBN: 978-1-5043-7808-6 (hc)
ISBN: 978-1-5043-7807-9 (e)

Library of Congress Control Number: 2017905069

Balboa Press rev. date: 04/21/2017

# Contents

# Dedication

I dedicate this book to Cubby, my current canine companion and an extraordinary spirit. Cubby has been my inspiration and constant support while writing this book. Thank you, Cubby, for reminding me of the true meaning of patience, forgiveness and unconditional love. Your energy and remarkable intelligence have earned you the name of "my Phenom."

*I love you huge*!

# Acknowledgements

Writing a book was never something I anticipated doing. It was a journey far outside of my comfort zone that would not have been accomplished without the help of many along the way.

My family has encouraged me and backed me throughout my life. My parents taught me what love is, and how to share it. My sisters are my best friends, and my brothers my greatest supporters. Each addition to our family has brought a new gift or helped to remind me of one I'd forgotten in myself. My love for all of you is far beyond words.

My dear friend Ed was beside me for over twenty years, and has passed beyond the veil of this life. He opened my eyes in so many ways through the struggles and adventures of the time we shared. Ed, I love and miss you, and often feel your presence beside me. Thank you for continuing to stand with me and support me along my way.

It was a difficult decision to do anything with this information and Sue Corrigan was there encouraging me to get going. Thank you, Sue, for your foresight, support and encouragement.

Debra Alford saved me from myself and edited this book. I'm so grateful to her for sharing her expertise and finding all those little things I failed to see—even after reading this many, many times.

The animals in my life have not only been ambassadors of love, but have sustained me during my most difficult times. This book is from and for them. To Cubby, Kaelie, Jamie, Aladdin, Fame, Thumper, Tsunami, Nikki, Brinks, Gamut, Jeepers, Shenanigans, Wish, Dream, Gentry, Szuma, Casey, Pax, Phoebe, Rebel, Scout, Pips, Saucy, Romeo, and all the incredible spirits who have shared their true unconditional love with me, I give you my eternal gratitude and love. I honestly believe our family nightly saying:

"Together forever, no matter wherever."

To every bit of creation, which is always there to uphold me and greet me with surprises and peace, I am forever grateful.

*God wrote two books, creation and scripture, and God would not have written the second if we were aware of his presence in the first.*

—St. Augustine

# Introduction

## The Early Years

As a child, I wanted nothing to do with animals and nature. Dogs scared me, cats made me sneeze, and our parakeet would barely miss me as she flew by. That would cause a scream nearly every time. My idea of fishing was getting my brother to bait my hook and then take off the fish if I caught one (he's always been a great brother). As a Girl Scout I tried camping, but spiders made me want to scream, mosquito bites drove me nuts, and the thought of confronting a skunk–well, that was absolutely terrifying.

It took decades for those walls to start to crumble, and a little Dutch Dwarf bunny started that change in 1990. Getting a rabbit was not my idea. A friend of mine brought me along to a pet store with her the Saturday before Easter and went on about the fate of this bunny if I didn't intervene. She hit a soft spot, and that's where a major change in my life began.

I had that bunny, named Thumper, for seven years. I loved holding him, and never wanted to put him down.

He had other ideas though, and would wiggle when he wanted me to let go. I often pushed to hold him a little longer and then he would make his message absolutely clear by peeing on me. Sometimes it was worth it for that extra snuggle. But for the most part I learned to respect his wishes.

## What Next?

Thumper died unexpectedly in 1998, and I was not prepared for what to do after he was gone. I thought I would get another bunny, but my friends thought otherwise.

My dear friend Ed decided we should visit a local shelter to just *look* at the dogs there. I had always been so afraid of dogs I thought this would be a futile effort. At the very end of a long row of cages sat a small puppy. The tag said she was a Sheltie, which was a word I had never heard before. There was something very sweet about her face, and yet she looked so small and frightened.

Ed somehow persuaded me to ask about her, and I found myself adding my name to a list of people for possible adoption. I was number six on the list, yet at 8:30 the next morning I got a call to pick her up. I was chosen because I had a fenced-in yard.

When I arrived at the shelter they told me it would be a good idea to get a crate for the puppy. Given my vast experience with dogs, I thought that I needed to go to the supermarket and get an orange crate. I pictured all the TV scenes with puppies sitting in that type of a crate while being pulled in a wagon. Luckily, the shelter had an appropriate crate available for Kaelie, and the shelter associates were able to contain their laughter (at least while I was there).

Kaelie and I started that awkward adjustment period which was a struggle for both of us. I found a book about Shelties which stated that it was important for them to have a strong alpha to follow. In my continuing ignorance, I went to the pet store to buy one. The clerk quickly found some basic training for us.

Kaelie (I called her K) opened a new chapter in my life. Having a dog brought experiences and opened doors I never knew existed. It wasn't long after I got K that I realized that she really had a lot more energy than me. So Jamie (I called her J), another Sheltie, was brought into our lives. It wasn't long before she was comfortable being part of my family.

K, J and I found agility and obedience competition. While enjoying the fun that brought us, our bonds grew deeper and stronger. Since I was single and childless, they soon became my kids (you know how that is). Some called them spoiled; I've always called them loved.

Then (somehow, while I wasn't looking) two more beautiful Shelties—Aladdin and Fame—joined my family, for a total of four wonderful kids. I lived with more fur than I could control and more love than I could have ever imagined. Each dog, with his or her unique personality and charm, found their own special place in my heart.

# From Happiness to Heartbreak

I had lost family members before, and had suffered pain and grief. But in 2009 J and Aladdin died five months apart. I considered Aladdin my heart dog, and losing him on my birthday felt like my heart was torn from my chest.

Losing two of my kids brought a pain I couldn't ease. I became severely depressed for months. During that time K and Fame stood by my side, loving and caring for me in every way they could. They patiently waited for me to realize they were there, and that I had two incredible spirits I could still touch and hold and share my life with. I was busy thinking that they would just be better off without me.

I believe that it was by the grace of God that I eventually got active again in the areas they enjoyed most—pet therapy and something called rally obedience (a different kind of obedience training). They were shining stars, beacons of love and life, touching others along their way.

Due to their incredible intelligence and adventurous spirits they were dubbed "Trouble" and "Double Trouble" at the veterinary hospital we frequented. Fame would mastermind a way to access the treasure and then share the loot with K, who I expect was right by her side acting as the lookout. They became extremely close to each other and to me.

That sharing was brought to a new depth in 2011 when I found they both had cancer. Both had progressed to the stage where palliative measures were all I could provide.

I felt helpless to do anything for them so I learned animal Reiki to try to comfort them in their distress. My heart broke when I would see them struggling. Fame passed in October (barely two years after Aladdin), and K died just ten days later. K was lost without Fame, and it did seem appropriate for them to be together this way. To say that I was devastated would be an understatement. I honestly think I lived in shock during the days that followed, uncertain of my future, and with no desire to continue living without them.

## A New Light – A New Direction

My life shifted again when a wide-eyed, shaved, slightly emaciated little dog grabbed my attention as I browsed through pictures of rescue dogs on the internet. It felt like those eyes saw deep into my spirit. He lived halfway across the country, and I had never met him—but I felt drawn to him like I had known him forever.

I arranged transportation for Cubby to be brought from Illinois. Cubby and I became family, and a new direction was set for both of our lives. He is with me today (as I write this), and is joined so closely to me that it leads some people to say we must have been cloned.

Cubby is an incredibly huge spirit stuffed into the little body of a Shih Tzu. He is a remarkable presence not only to me, but to everyone who crosses paths with him. He certainly is a phenomenal gift to me.

# Unexpected Messages

I don't remember exactly how long ago this happened, but one morning while having a cup of coffee, I was drawn to pick up a pen and paper. From there, it was like someone else had control of my arm. I could feel the movement of the pen and the strain of my muscles – but letters, making words that were not my own, were being written on the paper at a speed I could barely contain.

I was writing a letter from a deceased relative that needed to be sent out immediately. I really had no idea what I had written, so I asked if I could read it for spelling and grammar before I sent it. I was clearly told (with love) that it was not written to me and was basically none of my business. I was also told that I needed to get it out immediately. So I went to the post office while still in my pajamas, feeling pressured to complete my task.

I honestly have no recollection of what I wrote, but I know that its recipients appreciated that letter.

Similar requests to deliver messages or flowers from deceased relatives have become fairly common for me. Each time one has come to me, I experience self-doubts and a fear of rejection.

I have learned from these experiences that I am simply the connection for these messages. I remove myself as much as I can to make the messages as pure from their source as possible. To this date, the reactions have been positive and appreciative, though I hold my breath with each communication.

# Animal Communication

I've always had an interest in animal communication. I wondered if the ideas and feelings I experienced were actually from my dogs communicating with me. I wondered if I was imagining everything, hoping for it all to be real. I do know that I felt and continue to feel a special connection with animals, especially with my pets.

I started trying to communicate with my dogs, as the books I found instructed. Every resource I reviewed stated that anyone could do this—it was all a matter of practice and persistence.

I know that my meditation practice played a big role in enhancing my ability to communicate. After a fall down the stairs to my basement in April of 2013, I felt like my brain had changed (in addition to my inability to lift my head from the pillow.) Nothing ever showed up on the tests I received, but I believe the bouncing of my head on the stairs altered something. All of a sudden I could clear my mind instantaneously. Previously I struggled with trying to calm my mind. Now I could easily hold a state of wordlessness, and meditate for hours. This brought an incredible feeling of connection with God and all of creation.

This amazing gift I'd been given changed my life in so many ways. In particular, it was the catalyst for this book. When I would clear my mind I would often try to connect with Cubby. In doing so, the bond between us grew stronger and deeper each time.

I would try to test our communication at times, by asking Cubby to give me a kiss. I would hold that picture and thought in my mind—and he would understand! He'd come and give me the most gentle, loving kiss possible (which would make me just melt, of course.) I tried that often because I would still doubt myself and found it hard to believe—especially in the beginning. I drove Cubby to the point of just giving me sighs, as if to say "you have got to be kidding, another one!" Over time, I came to trust our communications more and more.

## This Book

One day in June of 2014 Cubby and I were sitting together on the floor. I was holding a journal I had just bought; its cover title read "Everything I Know I Learned from My Dog." Before I knew it, I picked up a pen and this book was written, through my communication with Cubby. It was like he was translating a message from animals I considered my kids, along with all the animals that have touched my life, and all of nature which I've taken for granted. Cubby blended the messages of the giant redwood and expansive rain forests with the delicate buttercup and single rose. He brought together the messages of the elephant and lion with those of the kitten and koala bear. Sometimes these messages have the tone you might expect from sweet, cuddly little Cubby. At other times, though, the messages take on a more massive tone, like what you might expect from a gorilla or tiger. There are also parts that include ideas I feel were clearly Divine messages. These all meshed throughout the communication.

Cubby gave *so* much for these messages. For two days after we finished he slept, barely awakening to eat a bit. I thought I was losing him for sure. He got through that, but was never the same. Around Christmas of that year I found out that he had become diabetic. Then he developed Cushing's disease and went blind—all in less than six months. Before the book he was in excellent health, even a bit overweight. Now I had to fight to keep weight on him. Cubby has given his *all* for this. I, on the other hand, have been dragging my feet to release it due to my own trepidations. There is also my intense fear that Cubby's mission here will be complete when this is published.

This book is a series of communications similar to what I have received from others in the past. I believe that it was presented from the perspective of a dog because that was a form I was intimately connected with and could easily translate. All of the lessons were given in an incredibly short period of time. I would hear a topic for a lesson and wonder if I was mistaken; how could what I was hearing and writing be making any sense? But as each lesson unfolded, I found it would weave into a message with profound wisdom that has never ceased to amaze me. At times I could barely hold the pen as my fingers cramped, but the writing continued. After each lesson was written, I had no recollection of what I had scribed, and it felt new as I read it later. The whole experience has been beyond amazing, beyond comprehension of how this could be coming through *me*.

The following pages speak for plants, animals, and all of God's creations. They convey a message of love and wisdom gathered and held for thousands of years.

My part here is to convey these messages to you as purely as I received them. I have tried to articulate words for their meanings as well as the emotions and wisdom they are meant to represent.

I know that what has been given to me is far too important for me to back away from. Am I afraid of rejection—especially from family and friends? *Absolutely!* Am I looking to get famous? *No way!* But there is something much larger than myself at work here. I realize that I cannot control the thoughts and beliefs of others but I can present ideas and suggestions for their consideration.

We (Cubby et al) ask that you read with an open mind and an open heart. Anyone can dispute or deny any part (or all) of this book, and that is each individual's choice. All we ask is that you read this in a spirit of light and love, because that is the way it is being sent. Take what resonates with you and embrace that part. Maybe try to expand a little and consider the parts that don't resonate. Regardless of the source, this is a message of *love*.

I hope this work finds a way to make a bit of difference somewhere, because it has brought my life new meaning and purpose. I have been given a new perspective from this experience, and from that I am honored to bring this message to you.

*But ask the animals, and they will teach you; or the birds in the sky, and they will tell you; or speak to the earth, and it will teach you; or let the fish in the sea inform you. Which of all these does not know that the hand of the Lord has done this? In his hand is the life of every creature and the breath of all mankind.*

—Job 12, 7-10 (NIV)

# Lesson 1

# We Are All Connected

*D*o you think if your name was Pistachio it would be cute, nice, weird, or maybe awesome? Then so would Max, Jane, John, Sunshine, Grace... Do you get my drift? What's in a name? It's a way to identify you. Way back, humans used names like Samson, meaning Sam's son. You've gotten much more creative in naming each other. You look at a baby to make sure the name "fits." You check the initials to make sure they don't spell something you consider bad. A. C. had an uncle whose initials were R. A. T. Probably not the best choice, but he found a way to take the name and not be defined by it.

You have so many names for—I'll use the word God. He is our Creator, Father, the One, the Source, Allah, Abba ... All of those names invoke a picture, a feeling or maybe some rationalized thinking in you. But the name I chose, God, doesn't define "him."

Likewise, negating the word God—or some other name like Buddha or Source—serves no purpose. How you chose to embrace and connect doesn't matter. The word to embrace is *love*. That matters! Hurting and even killing each other over names really makes no sense. If I had a hand, I'd scratch my head over the way humans act to express love with hurt.

Dogs will usually fight to protect their guardians or to get something they need, like food. We also fight because you train us to fight each other for our own survival. Please stop! That is part of humanity that disgraces itself. Disrespect for life of all kinds is a disrespect of our Creator and it is an attack on your very own essence. You hurt and detract from yourselves when you hurt life of *any* kind (except for your own survival needs—food, shelter and water.) Remember, we're all connected. We share the same essence. You don't see it, but you *are* hurting yourselves, and the generations to come.

Greed has brought down empires in the past. Do you think that humanity is now beyond causing the same catastrophes from your greed? If you think yes, think again—and again. See the destruction you cause from greed. See the love you dismiss from greed. See your babies with little future, due to greed.

A need for power is the same as greed. There is just *no* good outcome from greed. Its very nature is destruction, and so many humans can't see what they are doing.

Come down here and look up. Hopefully you will someday gain a new perspective of life. Try including not only a human viewpoint but also the perspective of all of us who speak a language you have forgotten. You get excited at the thought of communicating with aliens from other planets. How about getting excited about communicating with life on your own planet?

All of life is speaking, but you so often don't get it. At the end of your lives (for most of humanity) you will pass on without experiencing one of God's most precious gifts—hearing the voice of all creation. Hear our messages, because we have them too! If you don't listen, you'll miss out on hearing the voice of God in and through us. Don't make that mistake—it's like when you're not paying attention to what you are doing, so you end up stepping in poop!

*Humankind has not woven the web of life. We are but one thread within it. Whatever we do to the web, we do to ourselves. All things are bound together. All things are connected.*

—Chief Seattle

# Lesson 2

# Everything Has a Purpose

*S*ome people think that dogs, cats, and pets in general have it made. We eat, sleep, play, poop, and have wonderful lives—at least those of us in homes and not on the streets or terrified in a shelter. But we *don't* have it "made," as you would say. Think of it: Do you have any idea how hard it is to go outside to pee when it's snowing or when the yard is frozen? You want us to control our bodily functions and eliminate on demand. Many of you have trouble peeing in a cup when you go to the doctor's office!

I'm getting a bit off track. My point here is that you don't realize the expectations and pressures you put on us. Many of you take out your frustrations on us. You might have a bad day at work, so you ban us from being with you—"Put the dog outside, I don't want him slobbering around me," or "Get that cat away from me, she's shedding," etc.

Do you realize that humans shed too? You get your hair in our food, but we are grateful for the food, and we eat it anyway. We may get in your way, usually because we want to be close to you, and you push us away or pick us up and physically move us away from you. You step on our paws or tails, and we lick them and try again to be close to you. By the way, it's extremely stressful to never know when you are going to be physically picked up and relocated—usually to somewhere you don't want to be.

We might go for a walk with you and find something that grabs our attention, and we become intrigued. Do you have any idea how much information there is on a fire hydrant? It's similar to how you get enthralled by your computers and don't want to get off. Anyway, if you call and we don't come right away, many of you yell at us, and sometimes even hit us. And then you wonder why we don't want to come the next time you call.

We learn from experience. Animal brains do not rationalize like people's do. We learn by doing, sometimes over and over again until it becomes second nature. Hmm, don't many people do that too? We are not so different, and yet we are. We stand by you and love you regardless of how you treat us (there are exceptions to everything, including humans). We'll still try to protect you. We'll still greet you at the door or jump ecstatically when you come home.

We are unconditional, and so is our Creator. We try to soothe you, calm you, protect you, and love you. But we need your understanding, patience and trust, just as you ask of us. We are *of* love, just as you are, so let's share that instead of you trying to dominate and control us.

Humans and animals are here for each other, regardless of whether the animal is domesticated or not. Every single part of creation has a purpose, even if you cannot see it. Why do you judge if our lives are worthwhile or not? You have no idea of our mission—of why God put us in this place at this time. You play God when you hurt or slaughter animals for fun. You play God when you kill us in shelters because you think we are not worth anything. To some of you, we are a bother in your eyes.

Animals filled this earth long before humans, and yet we restrained from harming you, for the most part. You destroy plants and trees because they are in your way.

You throw away flowers because parts have died, not giving the rest a chance to bloom. And you put all of this life in plastic bags so it will not return to the earth for a hundred years or more (probably much more). Often the plastic goes into the oceans where it strangles the life out of God's creations there. You take us all for granted. You minimize our value and destroy whatever you please.

Why do you have so little regard for life? Maybe you need to change your definition of life to be inclusive of all of God's creations. Listen when you cut down a tree—you will hear its cry. You have diminished the earth. You have trampled on God's creations with no regard. All of this is catching up with humanity. You have less and less water to drink, clean air to breathe, and nourishing food to eat.

Do you not see how we are all connected, interrelated, and dependent upon each other? We non-humans cannot support you if you don't support us. What you take from us you take from yourselves. God made it that way. He cares for each of his creations, not only the ones walking upright on two legs. If you don't realize this soon, and live accordingly, you will destroy your future. The future of the earth and humankind is in the balance. Look beyond yourselves and see the whole.

*We are not apart from nature,*
*we are a part of nature. And to*
*betray nature is to betray us,*
*to save nature is to save us.*

—Prince Ea

# Lesson 3

# Look Up!

*D*o you realize how much time dogs spend with our necks bent back to look up at things? Compared to humans, we are somewhat small. We need to push our necks back to see just about everything. One of the best things in life is a good neck massage—it's even better than a butt scratch (close second to a belly rub, in my humble opinion). I think that when you look up at things, it gives you a unique perspective that is not available to those who spend their time looking straight—and it's far better than the perspective of those who always look down.

People spend so much time looking straight at each other. They give each other a quick going over and then form an opinion. Based on that opinion, they find something to judge as "less than" (or "more than") and may start looking at that person as inferior in some way. You think that makes you superior, and you live based on that opinion. Stop a minute and think about it—you judge in an instant. It goes beyond what you call racial profiling— it's people, animal, creation profiling. So many of you spend your time finding ways to feel "above" each other, while others are even finding ways to feel "less than" each other.

A. C.'s dogs have spent countless hours with the feeling of "less than" filling the room. She never said it aloud, but the depression, anxiety, hurt, and anger that plagued A. C. were devastating to her and broke her companions' hearts. All they could do was to be with her, offering kisses and showing her love. Many humans write us off as just "good dogs," but we are *so* much more. (That will be in a future discussion, so back to A. C.) She couldn't see the spirit that they could see. All A. C. could see was that "she wasn't..." Hours, days, weeks, months, years were spent in a crazy cycle of emotional and physical pain.

And for those people who find ways to feel superior to your brothers and sisters, you are suffering too. I think the need to feel superior is an attempt to ease the deeper issue of feeling inferior. You think you need to find a way to feel good, and that often comes from feeling above others in every way you can. All of these thoughts and decisions are generally made without your realization. I'm not judging you here. I'm just trying to bring awareness of the way you live.

Humans suffer from these crazy opinions of each other. It is all based on limited knowledge, regardless of how well you think you know someone. So try bending your head back and looking up for a different perspective. You may see the ceiling. That's not a limitation; consider it as protection. It's shelter from the elements.

You may see a crystal-clear blue sky. It is endless, and you are too! You may see clouds—some may be grey, and others white. The grey clouds bring rain, and fill your need for water. (By the way, grey is a beautiful color! It is the color of A. C.'s hair underneath that coloring she uses. Why do people want to hide it?) The white puffy clouds bring lightness, and can be in shapes that you can enjoy for hours.

You may see the dark sky of night. Darkness isn't bad; it can be peaceful and soothing. It can lead you to rest and be comforting. You may see the stars. They are reminders that the past is present. They are light that was created years and years ago that is only reaching the earth now. The present is the future—what is being created by those stars now will light the skies in the future. The past, the present and the future come together as one in the now. And the *now* is all we really have. Why are you wasting it comparing yourselves to each other, judging not only each other, but all of creation—including dogs? (Don't forget that you named us dog, which is God spelled backwards. We need to be treated with respect and love too.)

You may not consider animals and nature to be created in the image and likeness of God (as some of you believe humans are), but we are of God. The Father, the Creator, the Source lives in us—as in humans and as in every bit of creation. We are *all* connected, regardless of appearance. The basic element of every bit of creation is *love*. Stop and think about that for a moment. *All* of creation is made of love; we are all the same in this way. Why do you need to compare yourself to anything? We are all the same!

And I did say *we*. I want to speak for those of us who cannot be heard. When I say that we are all the same, I speak for plants, animals, the sky, the earth, and all of creation. Your scientific research is just now starting to glimpse the many complexities and commonalities we share. Go ahead, research, look, test. Do all the things humans need to do to understand everything around you. You are in for a thrilling ride of discovery and awe. But the bottom line that you will eventually find is that we are essentially the same; that we are all of the same essence. That essence is *love*. That essence is God, the Source, the Creator, whoever or however you choose to express it.

*It's not only moving that creates new starting points. Sometimes all it takes is a subtle shift in perspective, an opening of the mind, an intentional pause and reset, or a new route, to start to see new options and new possibilities.*

—Kristen Armstrong
(Two-time Olympic
Gold Medal cyclist)

# Lesson 4

# Come Together

*W*hy won't you let your pets go to church with you? We often hate it when you leave for church and we can't come. Are you afraid we'll see something we shouldn't? Are you afraid we'll bark or make a noise at the wrong time? We pray too you know! We usually don't poop on the floor; we try to be polite. We have respect and manners (if you have shown us). We want to see and experience the way you express your love of God (I chose to use the word God; change it as you wish). We (non-humans) want to feel that love; we want to be a part of your community.

I just realized that I'm using the word love often. *We love God too*! We want to share God's love that flows through us. We thank God for all he does and has given us. We'd just like to be a part of all the ways you express your love for our Creator. We're not partial to any religion. A. C. is Catholic and often goes to Mass. When she can't go to the building, she says she is doing church at home. She often watches Mass on TV, so I get a glimpse of what is done. But I can't feel the love that way.

By the way: Why do Catholics never say that you love God during your service? You dance around with words like praise, worship, and adore which all imply love. All the definitions of these words contain the word *love*. Why can't you just say "we love you" to God during your Mass? My take is that humans have a fear of some four-letter words, like love.

I digressed there. My point is that coming together is a wonderful way to feel and express your love and awareness of our Creator. You should also reflect on your sameness which goes beyond the church walls—regardless of the type of beliefs you have. We are all connected to each other and to the "One." Humans need to feel things emotionally to embrace them, to let something become part of their daily lives. Don't leave your love in the building. You unite so you can share in and feel God's love—so bring it out in how you live. It's how you live, not how you believe, that is the important piece. Yes, I just used the word piece (A.C. just questioned me on it as she is writing). It is the most important *piece*, because it is how you will find *peace* in your heart, mind, spirit, and in all of creation.

Outside, in nature, is our church. It has no walls. It accepts every living being. No judgments; it embraces. Walk in the woods and feel the trees hug and protect you. Stand in the ocean and feel the power of the seas. By the way, the seas accept everything. Would you please stop putting your garbage in them? That's just plain disrespectful.

Join in nature's church to feel God's love and share it with his creations. We all need love. Regardless of what you believe, you will eventually find that plants, animals— every part of creation—all thrive on love. We feel it. Yes, plants feel it too! You just need to expand your definition of the word feel. Humans will catch on, eventually. I'm here to give you a heads up about our perspective of *being*. We're different than humans—does that really matter?

*This is my simple religion.*
*There is no need for temples, no*
*complicated philosophies. Our*
*own brain, our own heart is our*
*temple, the philosophy is kindness.*

— Dalai Lama

# Lesson 5

# Act From Your Heart

You may not know what life is like in a big city like New York, but whether it's a city, a town, a neighborhood or whatever, it is living with a group of people close together (maybe closer than you like). That means getting along, giving each other space and hopefully helping each other out.

If you look at a colony of ants, or bees working in their hive, you will see they all work with a common goal. They do this by instinct; they support each other and thrive together. Humans have instincts to care for each other too. Many of you deny those instincts. You become obsessed with your own welfare, your power and your prestige. You deny your intuition that draws to mind the importance of the person sitting beside you, be it in the boardroom, on a bus, in a classroom, or at a dinner table.

You have forgotten what the ants and bees know: You need each other to thrive. All need to share in the responsibilities, labors, and fruits of those labors. When you are born, you are *all alike*. You are pristine in nature, a creation of the hand of God. Everything is new. You are *all equal* in essence. You need a leader, or queen bee, to help organize and provide order. But the leaders are no better and no worse than those whose lives they have taken responsibility for. In the eyes of our Creator, each of his creations—each soul—is equal. Each is precious and deserves happiness in this life. You are here to experience love in every way, shape, and form possible. You are not here to promote your happiness at the cost of others.

You often use the word "common" in an almost demeaning sense. Yet it holds the truth and substance of your relationships. Each of you, though different in body, shares a *common* bond. You share the same origin. You are made of the same substance as each other. You are all made from the essence of love from our Source. When you look at each other, don't look at the differences—look at what you have in *common* and build your relationships from there. Your relationships will be stronger and discrimination will be forgotten. You are all a single city on earth. You are *one* community in the eyes of God. You are responsible for each other.

When one of you thrives, it raises all of you. When one of you is hurt, you are all diminished. You have to see each other beyond your appearances, beyond your beliefs, beyond your "position" on earth. You are all the same. You all need to work together to thrive. You need the help and support of *all* nature to live as you are meant to.

Nature is also a creation from our Source. It is of the same essence. It has energy and vitality it shares with you, and you rarely notice it is there. The trees give you oxygen. Why do you cut down so many when there are multiple alternatives for shelter? If you would recycle all the paper you use there would be no need to end so many of their lives. Yes, they are *very much* alive and they contribute to your existence. They are among the oldest of the earth's vegetation, yet you disregard them. But then again, look at how often you disregard so many of the older people around you. So I guess I shouldn't be surprised.

Take a look at your family. Do you love and care about them? Now expand your concept of family to include your town, your country, the earth and all of creation. Do you love and care still? You may think that the concept is too big for you to contribute in a way that matters. You are so wrong in that mindset. The smallest action can reap the greatest benefits. What does it matter if you can see the results before you?

If you are working for the common good it will not matter if you see the benefits. Receiving praise and recognition for actions is not necessary. You know what you do: good or bad, kind or hurtful, selfish or generous. Act as if your actions are being done to yourself. Would you do it then? Would you do it to or for those who mean the most to you? Would you do it to or for our Creator?

Stop doing things in the name of God when they are hurtful, hideous acts you are committing. Do things from your soul—your inner self that is created of *love*. Some of you kill in the name of God. Would you approve of it if the victim was your parent, family or any of those you cherish and love? What if you were to be the victim? Would you approve of it then?

In nature we kill to survive. Humans do not need to kill each other for food. Cannibalism is long gone as a way of survival. What is wrong with your thinking? Animals are more civil than some humans. If each and every one of you would live from your heart there would be no need to kill or hurt each other. Your perception of life is distorted. You need to support, not ravage each other. You need to help each other, not raise yourselves up at the expense of each other.

It is time to change. It is time to teach your children to see from their hearts. It is time to ensure that your actions (and the actions of others who imitate you and learn from you) are all done from your heart. The change may seem difficult at first, but it will soon become routine, and you will be acting from your heart without having a debate in your head.

Remember, you are all *"common!"*

*Let us dream of tomorrow where
we can truly love from the soul,
and know love as the ultimate
truth at the heart of all creation.*

—Michael Jackson

# Lesson 6

# Cherish the Animals

*D*o you care for a dog, a cat, a fish, a gerbil, or a rhinoceros? Yes, a rhinoceros. I'm using a rhinoceros to help make my point a little more easily. If you cared for a rhinoceros, it would be in a zoo or other appropriate habitat (I hope). You would take care of its needs and possibly grow fond of it—maybe even build a relationship with it. You would not consider a rhinoceros to be your possession, would you? It is God's creation and belongs to the world as you do.

Why do you then consider dogs, cats, rabbits, fish, gerbils, etc. to be your possessions? They are living beings, brought into your life, which you chose to care for. You take responsibility for their welfare. You are their guardians, their protectors, and their caretakers. They are not things like this piece of paper. And in essence, you don't even own this piece of paper. You are using it in a transient way and hopefully it will continue on for the good of others. It came from a living, breathing tree. Yes, you know, carbon dioxide in and oxygen out. That's like your breathing, just in reverse.

Anyway, all of God's creations are here to be cared for by you. And it *is* your responsibility to care for us (pets), and the trees, oceans, sky, etc... Don't think of your neighbors as "weird" or "bleeding hearts" because they care. They are a blessing. They are living as you are meant to. Caring in every sense of the word is essential for your survival. Those creations that are unable to care for themselves are your responsibility (including your disabled and elderly). Those creations that you are hurting and destroying are your responsibility.

Dogs are sometimes left outside in a yard to fend for themselves all day, regardless of the weather or time of year. They are neglected and are slowly dying due to a lack of caring. We hurt in the way you do. We feel in the way you do. We love in the way you do. So do all of God's creations. We may not fit your definitions of hurt or love or of being alive. So, *fix your definitions*, and expand your minds. It's not hard. We have done it in order to understand and accommodate you.

Things are most often not totally as they seem on the outside. There is more substance, more complexity within. Even if you haven't found a way to prove it yet, all life still feels. Once again, just fix your *definition* of feeling. It's very evident to us. I guess we see things from a different perspective—a broader, more encompassing perspective.

Remember to look up and see from a new perspective. You will find yourself thinking with new possibilities. If seeing is believing, then keep looking until you see. Think of how hard it is for fish to see you through a fish bowl. You are distorted, maybe even dark and fuzzy, due to the condition of the water. You need to change that water and clean the bowl every so often for the fish to thrive. You need to "clean your glasses" (so to speak) every so often for you to thrive.

*We must fight against the spirit of unconscious cruelty with which we treat the animals. Animals suffer as much as we do. True humanity does not allow us to impose such sufferings on them. It is our duty to make the whole world recognize it. Until we extend our circle of compassion to all living things, humanity will not find peace.*

—Albert Schweitzer

# Lesson 7

# It All Comes Down to Love

*L*ove is better than a treat or a toy or a bone. It is a treat of the most amazing kind. It nourishes you and allows you to thrive. It heals, softens, and embraces.

Love is patient. Talk about patient—to be a dog you need to have the patience of a saint (as you would call it). You have no idea what we have to live with! We get bopped, kicked, stepped on, and have things fall on us (or close by). These may not be intended but they are reminders of your humanness. And that's what makes A. C. so special. Her humanness thrives on love—so does my "dogness." She's horrified when these things happen to me because she has the most gentle and caring heart. Her gasp and "I'm so sorry!" when these things happen translates into "your life matters." She has said she would rather cut off her arm than purposely hurt us, and I believe her. That is love.

A. C. feeds me, but anyone can feed a dog. She takes me for walks even when I (or she) can't walk very well. But anyone can do that. She picks up my poop and sometimes gets it all over herself (yes I'm implying that she's klutzy), and she never complains. She doesn't yell—A. C. loves me. She'll do things for me that she won't do for herself. I (and all of our canine family) wish she truly knew, and deeply felt, how much we appreciate all the things she does. A. C. is love. She lives love. She spreads love. I am the privileged recipient of that love. She does everything in and of love. *That* is God, alive and breathing here. I know A. C. thinks that I'm the essence of love; she sees it in me. I wish and want her to see it in herself. She is the essence of love. So is *everyone* who is reading this.

As God's messenger I'd like to say: Look in the mirror, deep into your own eyes where your true self lives. Look into yourself and see the beauty there, the love that abides within you. *You* are a gift to be shared! *You* are the essence of love! *You* are the essence of God!

*Even*
*After*
*All this time*
*The Sun never says*
*To the Earth,*
*"You owe me."*
*Look*
*What happens*
*With a love like that*
*It lights the*
*Whole*
*Sky*

—Sufi Poet Hafiz

# Lesson 8

# Shit Happens!

*I*t's a part of everyone's life, so why be embarrassed by it? It's part of creation. It's inevitable, and actually healthy—it's destructive if you can't poop. As I hear you say, "shit happens." It happens to me and to you, to the birds, and all living creatures large and small.

If you take the word "shit" in a negative context, it means unwanted things—but you need it to be healthy. You need the unwanted, bad, hurtful things to treasure the good and to seek what's best when you are trapped in futility. That's where you learn life's lessons. It can be where you turn and realize the importance of reaching out to others. It can force you to wash off the bad stuff, to expose the good.

You use manure to grow food (recycling—great). Some dogs eat it. (I personally would have no desire to, but some animals do.) I think there is something these dogs feel they are lacking, so they are drawn to it. When you lack, when you crave, you are drawn to things that fill your needs. You are often drawn to make changes or to go after the things more appropriate for you. It can be the "kick in the butt" you need, because why else would you seek and grow?

Some people choose to stay stuck in shit. Some of you complain and pity yourselves over it, seeking sympathy for your "plight." Some of you take action, sometimes over and over again. A. C. says our motto is "We never give up!"

Animals accept what happens and move on. Some of us have to live without a limb, but we learn to thrive (some humans too). Some of our tails get cut, *not* including the ones you *intentionally* cut off. Why do you do that? You think that is the way a perfect specimen of a specific breed should look. Who are you to decide? God creates us with a long tail or floppy ears—that is the way God chooses. Who are you to change that? We are *all* perfection in our creation.

Why do you obsess over your perfection? Forget about staring in the mirror, looking at what you consider flaws in what our perfect Source has created. Open your minds and again *change your definitions*, for your own sakes as well as ours! We submit to your desires because we want to please you. Would you approve of someone else deciding to crop your ears because they think your ears should be different?

We should accept our differences and revel in them. It's what makes this world a beautiful and interesting place. You know you'd be bored if everything looked alike. Everything is exactly as it should be. Don't change us to fit your concepts and definitions. Change your definitions to be more inclusive!

Humans create those definitions and you can change them for us and for yourselves. Your body is perfect as you are! Your minds and some of your ways of thinking may need working on. We try to adapt to please you in every way. Your children often do the same. Practice *acceptance*—when you practice rejection you are rejecting *love*. Why do you insist on doing that?

*My happiness grows in direct proportion to my acceptance, and in inverse proportion to my expectations.*

—Michael J. Fox

# Lesson 9

# Try Silence

.

$S$ ilence is such a gift; I treasure it. A dog's hearing is much more developed than a human's. It was needed for survival at some point and is still needed, but not in the same way. We *can* hear a pin drop. We *can* hear your whispers. A. C. either doesn't realize that or forgets it. Whispering doesn't stop us from hearing; it makes us pay more attention. Remember how it was when you were a child and you strained to hear what adults were saying as they whispered? Or sometimes they may have spoken in another language and you fought to understand it? A whisper seems to hold a special message for humans, for whatever reason.

In the extremely noisy world humans have created, I think a whisper is a gift, much preferable to screaming. How do you do it? You have the TV talking at you, the radio playing music, and then you try to understand each other as you speak. No wonder you have so many misunderstandings. All of that noise distracts you from paying attention to the words that are important; those words of your parents, your friends, and even those of your thoughts. I find it extremely frustrating, and it wears me down. I can't even get some peace riding in the car with the music somehow always playing (or A. C. singing!)

I prefer silence, as you call it, yet I can still hear so much beyond that. A. C. has realized it's good to leave the TV and radio off when leaving the house. It gives my ears, and brain, a rest from trying to process it all. Why are so many of you afraid of silence? Why are you afraid of your thoughts? Are you afraid that you just might connect with God? You need the silence to hear him. You need to relax and enjoy the calmness around you. Humans need to learn how to "*be*"—that is to be with themselves and our Creator. In silence you will learn more important things than you see on TV. Your music can be soothing, or it can cloud your mind and senses to numb you from being one with this world.

Nature knows that we connect with God in the silence. It often appears to A. C. as if I'm "zoned out," or in a trance, which causes her concern. I'm not having a mild seizure or some other type of malady. I'm listening and connecting with our Source. God created this world with silence as the natural state so we all could hear his voice and connect with him.

Animals speak to each other when necessary, but they do not speak *at* each other with a barrage of meaningless sounds. We locate each other and warn each other with sounds. We have our own languages to convey love and support for each other. We communicate with each other most often through our actions. Humans have an expression about that: "Actions speak louder than words." So we speak loudly in silence. God speaks loudly in the silence. Nature speaks loudly in silence.

If humans stop and take a break to just *be*, you will learn to hear us all. It may take practice, or it may come naturally, but you will become aware of your surroundings and your world in a different way. You may even come to appreciate *all* of God's creations on this earth. Every living being has a message—a purpose for their life—and it is best shared.

We try to share, but we—meaning animals and the world you inhabit—are most often not heard. We try over and over again, but humans need to be still to hear us. And we in turn want to hear you. We can hear you best in the silence and in those important messages you convey when you whisper.

There is a place in the Bible you have written where it says that God was not heard in the noises, but rather in the whisper of the wind (paraphrased from 1 Kings 19:12). God's voice is in the whisper. Stop, and in the silence you will hear it.

*We need to find God and he cannot be found in noise and restlessness. God is a friend of silence: see the stars, the moon, and the sun, how they move in silence... We need silence to be able to touch other souls.*

—Mother Teresa

# Lesson 10

# You Choose

*C*onsider me Agent 001. Call me Bond—Cubby Bond! I've been watching you for years and now it is time to report some of my observations.

**To**: Humans

**From**: The Rest of God's Creations (per Agent Bond)

**Re**: Human Behaviors and Attitudes

From countless hours of observation and interaction, I have found the following:

Humans can love unconditionally. Most of you often choose not to because it is easier not to. Those who *do* love unconditionally know the inexplicable joy this kind of love brings. Remember that you most often draw to yourself what you embrace (some of you call it karma). It's easier said this way: You get what you give.

Humans stomp on nature. You destroy, remove, or kill anything that is in your way or may be annoying at that moment. Remember that you are destroying life for your own convenience. If you open your mind and heart, you will hear the suffering from a tree when it is cut down. You'll hear the agony in being shot and slowly dying so that you can cut off our heads and hang them on your walls. Why do you kill when it is not for food? You consider that fun and challenging. We see it as a direct attack on God and his creations. Nature, meaning plants and animals, will gladly give up their lives for your survival. But to kill for some convoluted pleasure should be considered premeditated murder.

Humans are changeable; you call it trainable for animals. You can adjust and embrace with ease if you choose. You have free will—the freedom to choose how you conduct yourselves. You can choose to kill, maim, and destroy; or to respect, embrace, and fortify. You do forget that your choices affect the whole. You can choose to diminish or to lift up all creation by your actions.

When you forget about us (meaning the rest of creation), you forget a piece of yourselves and the biggest part of God's creation. There is much more life outside of humanity than there is in the number of humans on this earth. You forget us in your race for money and power. You forget what you are doing to yourselves, and to generations to come. Everything that God creates has a purpose for the benefit of all. You need to see beyond yourselves and the current moment. You need to honor and respect *all* life, *all* of God's creations.

Respectfully submitted,

Agent 001

*If one day you have to choose between the world and love, remember: If you choose the world you'll be left without love, but if you choose love, with it you will conquer the world.*

—Albert Einstein

# Lesson 11

# Spread Your Wings

*B*irds of a feather flock together! That's for the birds! A little birdie told me! Boy, humans have used birds to reflect a lot of characteristics about themselves. For example: Birds of a feather flock together. Well yeah, birds often stay with their families, care for their kids, and teach them to fly. A sparrow has no desire to be around other birds that consider it to be food. Birds often stay together for protection. They understand each other's "tweets," being the originators of the idea of tweeting (yes, that's a joke).

So think about it, how are you as humans so different? Don't you prefer to be with like-minded people? You generally care for your children and teach them to read and to drive. Would you please teach them to stop for animals when driving and adopt that practice yourselves? You don't have the right to take our lives because you are in a hurry or are talking on your phone.

I realize that accidents happen, and you may not see us. You also take each other's lives for the same reason. But no creation deserves to die due to selfishness on your part. We don't deserve to die because you think we are in the way. If you were in a cougar's path would it be all right for him to take your life? Hardly. Please give us the same respect for our lives.

Back to hanging around together (flocking): it is easy to relate when you share ideas or experiences in common. It is easier to bond when you're alike in some way. So why do you so often use a phrase like "birds of a feather flock together" in a denigrating manner? Why do you think that we as non-humans would act differently than you? We care. We share. We protect. We help each other.

Some animals and birds may prefer to live independently, but so do some of you. We may need to nudge our children out of our nests—can you relate to that? When you say things about other creatures or any part of creation in a way that implies they are "less than," you are saying it about yourselves. When you say it about another human, do you not do the same? What leads you to believe that you are superior to all—especially to each other? We don't judge you; we leave that to God. We don't destroy you; we let you do that to yourselves.

And what does "that's for the birds" mean? You often feed them what you feel is unsuitable to eat yourselves. You kill them with pesticides you spray on your fruits and vegetables (that kill other creations of God). Do you really think that all the chemicals you put on nature or pour into the earth and sky won't in turn hurt you? The birds would like to request goggles to protect their eyes when they try to fly through the smog you create. Will humanity ever learn to care in time? What will it take to convince you that what you do to us affects you as well?

We are all part of the *whole*. We are all part of God and he cares about all of his creation. Our atoms are made of the same particles as yours. Why should they not be affected similarly?

You use the phrase "a little birdie told me." Do you mean that birds and you communicate? Nature still holds and understands God's language. It is humans who have forgotten how to communicate (in every way!) There are exceptions; some exceptional people choose to open their minds and hearts to connect. There are some, but there need to be many, many more if this planet is ever going to thrive. We need to work as one to flourish, or we are all hurt—*humankind and the rest of the world.*

You are not the only beings that inhabit this world but you are the only ones destroying it. You can change so much by adjusting a little for the benefit of all. Do you consider us worth it? If not, you choose the same for yourselves.

*Science cannot solve the ultimate mystery of nature. And that is because, in the last analysis, we ourselves are part of the mystery we are trying to solve.*

—Max Planck

# Lesson 12

# Remember the "kind" Part of "Humankind"

*H*umans see that some of us run very fast or jump very high. But do you realize the speed of your own actions and the possible results from them? For example, A. C.'s mind is constantly going from one thing to another, with her body changing directions. I most often am trying to follow her. I want to see what's going on; there may be something good coming my way.

Well, often humans' constant change of directions results in our tails being stepped on, our bodies getting kicked or our paws getting jammed. I've learned to try to anticipate the changes, trying to dance around the movements of your feet. I'm often not successful because my movements cause her to trip over me and we both get hurt.

All actions cause a reaction, a consequence of your action. Are you aware of the consequences you are causing from your actions? Often you can do something that is helpful to someone, but which in turn hurts someone else. Humankind has been blessed with incredible intelligence that translates into the actions you decide to pursue. Are you aware of how often your actions may result in transient good for you but permanent damage to the rest of God's creations?

Nature isn't able to stand up in front of you with protest signs to try to get your attention. We try to convey our messages but you don't see or hear us. We want to live on this wonderful planet in a healthy, vibrant way along with you. We give you everything we can, everything we are, often even our lives to promote your health and happiness. Why is it so hard for so many of you to care for us too?

My purpose here is to be the voice of nature, to let you become aware of the animals' cry. I am trying my best to do that. Animals and nature share so much with humanity, but through your actions you dismiss us as not important. You believe that your needs are of the utmost importance. Yes, God created humans to rule over this earth—over all of creation. And he wants you to love the rest of his creation as he does.

We exist for a reason. Your intellect allows you dismiss us, step on us and destroy us, without taking the time to evaluate the reasons we are here. Most of you don't understand our reasons for existence. You don't care to. So many of you live in this world and use it greedily for your benefit (at times) without thinking beyond yourselves in the now (most times).

You want your children to have a better life than you. You want them to live abundantly, to be happy, safe and healthy. Without caring for us you are diminishing their future. With your incredible intelligence can't you find solutions to your problems that benefit us as well? We are constantly changing, trying to adapt to your needs as you consume us. Please, can't you adjust a bit to allow the rest of creation to live as God created us? We share ourselves with you in our entirety, but we count on you for our lives. Can you maintain rather than destroy God's creations? Can you love us, while also loving yourselves?

The bottom line is that we are dependent on each other. When you carelessly destroy us, you diminish yourselves and your children's future. God created you not only to rule over the world but to care for it, to preserve it, to keep it alive. The word caretaker includes the word *"care,"* which is as essential to it as *"taker."* You need to take with care, to include love and compassion in all your actions.

We are made of the same essence as humankind. We share this world. Would you please remember the "kind" part of humankind? The bottom line comes down to love.

Please remember us when you act. We share our love for you. The energy of love is abundant—it is infinite. Please share that love with *us*.

*The heart is like a garden. It can grow compassion or fear, resentment or love. What seeds will you plant there?*

—Buddha

# Lesson 13

# Every Life Matters

What do you think happens to you when you die? Do you go to heaven or hell? Do you just stop being and dissipate into thin air? Do you meet your friends and family? How about animals, plants and the rest of God's creation? What do you think?

I *know* there's a Creator (God) that we come back to. I know God includes all of his creations; why wouldn't he? Are dogs loved less because they have tails? Humans have a tailbone—that's close enough for me. Dogs have four legs and you have two. Does God care about us less because we use four? We could walk on two legs, but choose not to. You could walk on all fours (as you put it), but you choose not to. Is that a reason we should be kept from the presence of our Creator, the Source of Divine love?

Divine love sounds all-inclusive to me. I know it is. The development of one's brain, body, or whatever physical forms doesn't matter to him. He loves all of his creations and welcomes all back to himself at the end of their journey.

Every living creation has a journey, a mission, something to add to this world that would diminish the world without it. Human embryos are made of the same living cells as you, and are alive in that way regardless of whether or not you choose to believe they are developed enough to be considered persons. I'm *not* here to debate that issue. My point is that the embryo, as it is made of living cells, has a mission. It touches other lives regardless of your definition of life. Its mission can last seconds or a hundred years, but the world would not be the same without its presence.

Plants and animals have a mission. You would not be here without us. The seas, sky, sun, all living cells join to make God's perfect creation. Do you believe that God is perfection? If so, how can you believe that any of his creations are less than perfect? He could only create perfection in each and every one of you, each and every animal, plant, etc. *Everything is perfect as created from a perfect God.* No creation's value should be diminished in your minds because it is not a human being.

You can't live on this planet without all the pieces God puts in place here. Every cell, atom, particle, quark or whatever name you give it is here because it originated from the same Source. Every bit of creation is an expression of love from God and deserves to be treated as such. Humans make up a part of this planet, but in terms of the universe, you are miniscule. Your feelings of superiority and grandness blind you to the fact that two tiny atoms colliding can propagate an effect that could destroy you all.

The next time you see some road kill, try thanking that creature for what it has added to this world. The world would not be the same without its presence, regardless of whether or not you know why it was here. How many people on the other side of the world know why, or even care why, you are here (and vice versa)? But each and every life matters.

Don't minimize the importance of your own lives either. You have no idea of the importance of the role *you* play in this world. A. C. thought she was a "nobody"—she often felt the world would be better off without her. If that had happened how would this book have been written? How would this message be given to humanity? And still she sometimes diminishes her worth and often questions why she is here.

Questioning the reason for something is not wrong; it is a healthy function of growing. But there comes a point where *trust* becomes the underlying factor. Humans want to be in control. You want to know how, when, where, why something is as it is. The rest of us let go and live in the moment. We never know what may happen or when, so we treasure this moment and trust that God will take care of the rest.

We know we are here for a relatively short period of time and then pass on back to our Creator. Some other creation will fill in where we left off. We are not afraid to die; we know it is a part of being here. That is part of God's perfect plan for his creation. It's a changing, growing, evolving creation. It pulses with the changes in every living thing. It is vibrant, expressive and growing in ways beyond comprehension. It is the changing seasons, the passing of the baton from the old to the young in all species. It is expanding and contracting as with each of our breaths. It is eternal, as we all are. It is the most glorious adventure each of us has undertaken. In the end, for all of us, it is perfect! Its essence is love. **It is God!**

*Never, never, be afraid to do what's right, especially if the well-being of a person or animal is at stake. Society's punishments are small compared to the wounds we inflict on our soul when we look the other way.*

—Martin Luther King

# Epilogue

## A bit of wisdom

There is only one way to connect deeply with nature of any kind—it is in stillness. You need to quiet yourself, listen and be with all that surrounds you. Be still with the animal you may be with. Any true communication requires listening as well as speaking. We hear you all the time, but you need to be still to hear us.

Humanity's world can be a jumbled mess of noise and confusion. The world of nature can be calm and peaceful. We welcome you to join our world, to immerse yourself deeply in our presence. We don't just welcome you; we *want* you to join us. Nature is not complete without you, as you are a masterpiece in God's creation.

Finding the time, place or circumstance to cultivate stillness may be difficult for many of you, so I offer you this:

> When you go to bed at night, picture the sky
> brightly filled with stars, and a gentle breeze
> caressing your face. There is stillness here, a
> peace that starts to transcend your being. Be
> mindful of that as it wipes away the cares

and struggles of the day, and concerns about tomorrow. Be still in this moment, and be open to the love that embraces you.

In the morning before your day fills with obligations and chaos, picture the most beautiful sunrise you can imagine, with the warm rays of the sun slowly coming forth and reaching to caress your face. Feel its warmth fill and brighten every cell in your body. Be still and absorb its energy and light. It is quiet and peaceful, and those feelings fill your body, mind and heart. Feel the warmth of that love embrace you and hold you through the day ahead.

In the stillness is the connection. With nature, there is a direct connection to the love and support of God. You are **never** alone in this world. We want you to feel our love for you, and God's love through us. We are here for you—anytime, day or night. Just be still and connect.

We will hold you to calm your fears. We will be present to support you in all your struggles, and light your way through the darkness you encounter. We want to rejoice with you when you are happy and stand beside you when sad. Be still and be loved.

Love,

Cubby et al

# Tribute

On November 2, 2015, my wonderful, sweet eyed, ever loving best friend was released to heaven. Cubby's little body was finally too ravaged to contain him and provide any semblance of who he was. When I took him to the vet on that day he could barely hold his head up. Then all of a sudden he raised his head looking straight up to heaven (I believe). His tail started to wag with such intensity it was pounding on my leg. He arched his back and was trying to jump up to the heavens. I literally had to hold him down. There was no doubt in my mind that he saw something and was trying to reach it (in spite of being blind!)

My teacher, friend, and soul mate is free and with the rest of my kids, tear-assing around heaven. Some of you reading this know the intense pain and grief that takes hold of you in this situation. I have it still, raw and deep, as I write this. Each of my animals has taken hold of a piece of my heart and remains there. Every time I lose one (or two) of my kids it feels like my heart shatters into those pieces and will never be put back together. And it feels like there's absolutely no room for another piece to be taken. The pain involved is so intense, and continues on to some degree for each of my kids.

Truth is though, I know, when the time is right, somehow, some way, my heart will expand to include more. That's the way love works. Love can't be contained. It's meant to be shared, and lasts for eternity.

# About the Author

*A*nne Tremblay has BA degrees in Mathematics and Managerial Economics. A head-first fall down her basement stairs in 2013 opened her ability to communicate with animals, nature, and individuals who have passed on. Meditation and Reiki have become an important part of her life. She lives in Cumberland, Rhode Island with her new dog Saucy.

Printed in the United States
By Bookmasters